BEN RASKIN

GROW

A family guide to growing fruits & vegetables

RB

Boulder

2017

Roost Books

An imprint of Shambhala Publications, Inc.

4720 Walnut Street

Boulder, Colorado 80301

roostbooks.com

First published in the UK in 2017 by

Leaping Hare Press

Ovest House, 58 West Street

Brighton BN1 2RA

United Kingdom

www.quartoknows.com

This book was conceived, designed, and produced by

Leaping Hare Press

Printed in China

10 9 8 7 6 5 4 3 2 1

First U.S. Edition

Distributed in the United States by Penguin Random House LLC and in Canada by Random House of Canada Ltd

Library of Congress Cataloging-in-Publication Data

Names: Raskin, Ben, 1969– author.

Title: Grow: a family guide to growing fruits and vegetables / Ben Raskin.

Other titles: Family guide to growing fruits and vegetables

Description: First U.S. edition. | Boulder, Colorado: Roost Books, 2017.

Identifiers: LCCN 2016030862 | ISBN 9781611804027 (hardcover: alk. paper)

Subjects: LCSH: Food crops. | Gardening. | Plants, Edible. | Fruit. | Vegetables.

Classification: LCC SB175 .R37 2017 | DDC 635—dc23

LC record available at https://lccn.loc.gov/2016030862

Contents

All about plants

In this book we will learn all about growing tasty fruits and vegetables from scratch, from preparing the soil and planting seeds to planning your garden and harvesting fruits and vegetables to cook a delicious recipe. Before we get started, let's find out more about what plants are and how they make the energy they need to grow big and strong.

What makes a plant a plant?

Plants contain a green substance called "chlorophyll." This captures carbon from the air and water from rain and, using energy from sunlight, converts these into sugars (food). This process, called "photosynthesis," is what makes plants special. Almost all animals rely on plants for their food. So life on Earth depends on photosynthesis.

FACT
Solar panels do the same job as plant leaves, transforming sunlight into energy for us to use in different ways.

PLANT STRUCTURE

Just like we have veins and arteries to move blood around our bodies, plants have tubes called "xylem" and "phloem" running up and down their stems and branches.

XYLEM moves nutrients dissolved in water up from the soil.

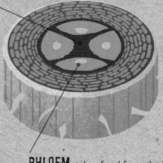

PHLOEM takes food from the leaves and transports it to all of the parts of the plant that need it.

SEEDS

FLOWERS

Seeds

Most plants make seeds to help them survive and spread. Pollen from the male part of the flower pollinates the female part of the flower, and this makes a seed. When it is ready, the seed falls from the plant and lands on the soil. Germination is when the seed sprouts a shoot and a root. The shoot grows up to the light looking for sunshine, while the root heads down into the ground.

These pretty flowers are all mine!

Roots

All plants have roots that anchor the plant and stop it from blowing over or away. They also bring water and nutrients to the plant. Roots usually grow into the soil, but some plants grow in places where there is no soil, such as in a tree or up a wall. As a general rule, a plant's roots are about the same size as the parts above ground.

Flowers

Most plants have flowers to help them make seeds. Although we may like the look and smell of flowers, they are not like that just for us to enjoy. Flowers attract the various creatures that will help take pollen from one plant to another. Insects are the most common pollinators.

ROOTS

What plants need to grow

Like us, plants need to respire (breathe), drink, and eat, but they don't do it in the same way as us. They can't move around to find what they need, so instead they have adapted to cope with using what is already there. Here's how they do it:

Feeding

To produce the sugar that they rely on, plants need:

CARBON Taken from carbon dioxide, a gas that is absorbed through holes in their leaves.

HYDROGEN In the water that is absorbed through plants' roots.

OXYGEN Found both in the air and in water.

ENERGY FROM SUNLIGHT To turn carbon, hydrogen, and oxygen into sugar (glucose), plants need energy. They take this from sunlight.

O_2

H_2O

$C_6H_{12}O_6$

CO_2

FACT

Plants can use their roots as well as their leaves to take in or release oxygen. A good soil structure will help them to do this.

$$6CO_2 + 6H_2O \qquad C_6H_{12}O_6 + 6O_2$$

CARBON DIOXIDE + WATER (IN THE PRESENCE OF LIGHT) = GLUCOSE AND OXYGEN.

PLANT NUTRIENTS

As we've seen, hydrogen, oxygen, and carbon are the essential chemical elements for photosynthesis, but which other nutrients do plants need to grow strong and healthy? The full periodic table shows all the chemical elements that have been discovered. Each element is given a number and a symbol. Here is a smaller version just for gardeners.

Feed your soil organisms with compost (see pages 14–15) to make sure that you have plenty of the essential nutrients, or try a liquid fertilizer (see page 17).

I bet these don't taste very nice!

7 **N** NITROGEN	15 **P** PHOSPHORUS	19 **K** POTASSIUM
12 **Mg** MAGNESIUM	16 **S** SULFUR	20 **Ca** CALCIUM

5 **B** BORON	17 **Cl** CHLORINE	25 **Mn** MANGANESE	26 **Fe** IRON
28 **Ni** NICKEL	29 **Cu** COPPER	30 **Zn** ZINC	42 **Mo** MOLYBDENUM

NITROGEN, PHOSPHORUS, & POTASSIUM Needed in large amounts and crucial to plant development—without enough of these, your plants just won't grow.

MAGNESIUM, SULFUR, & CALCIUM
Although not needed in such large amounts, these are still important for plant growth. Magnesium is esssential for photosynthesis.

MICRONUTRIENTS These are required in small amounts. Zinc and boron are needed to make seeds, while copper is important for photosynthesis.

HOW TO SPOT DEFICIENCIES

Some gardeners do a soil test to find out if they have any nutrients missing from their soil. However, you can also be a plant detective and look for clues on plant leaves. You need to be able to recognize the younger and older leaves on a plant. Older leaves are bigger, tougher, and nearer to the ground. Younger leaves are smaller and at the top of the plant.

Here are six common signs of nutrient deficiencies. If you spot one of these, use a liquid fertilizer like the one on page 17 to put nutrients back into your soil.

BORON Young leaves shrivel and die.

SULFUR Young leaves turn pale green or yellow.

MAGNESIUM Older leaves turn yellow, but the veins stay green.

NITROGEN Older leaves turn yellow or pale green all over.

FACT
Some plants have red or yellow leaves naturally, or their leaves change color in the fall, so make sure you know what color your leaves should be before you check them.

PHOSPHORUS Older leaves turn red or purple all over.

POTASSIUM The edges of older leaves go brown and dry.

Respiring

Plants have small holes in their leaves called "stomata" through which oxygen and other gases go in and out. Plants need oxygen to survive. They take it in all day and night and, like us, get rid of carbon dioxide as part of that process. However, they need carbon dioxide for photosynthesis, so during the day they also take in carbon dioxide and give out some oxygen.

Drinking

Plants mostly take up water through their roots. Some plants, such as chicory, have very deep roots to reach low down into the soil to find water. Others, such as cactus plants, have developed ways of storing water so that they can survive long periods with no rain. Almost all plants are able to live for some time without water, although when they have just germinated this might only be a couple of days.

A home

Most plants need to have their roots in the soil. As well as being their main way of getting water, this also keeps them "rooted" in place. Roots also take up the nutrients from the soil that the plant needs to be able to grow. Plants often work in partnership with fungi and other soil organisms, giving them sugar in exchange for the nutrients in the soil that the plants might not otherwise find. In fact, about half of the food that a plant produces is given away through its roots to soil creatures.

Hey! Where's my dinner?

The Seasons

In most parts of the world, the weather and length of day change during the year. This is because Earth spins around on a tilted axis. As it rotates around the sun, different parts of it move nearer or farther away from the sun. Plants have evolved to cope with this. Let's find out what this means for us as gardeners.

Knowing what to grow where

Seasons are different depending on where you live. At the equator, the weather doesn't change much during the year and it is generally warmer. At the North and South Poles, it is dark almost all day during the winter, light all day in the summer, and is much colder. Most of us live somewhere in between. If you understand your local seasons, you will know which plants you can grow and how to grow them better.

HOW PLANTS SURVIVE THE COLD

Many plants go to sleep over the winter as a way of coping with the cold. Different plants have found different ways of doing this:

PERENNIALS, such as asparagus and rhubarb, die back and hide underground. When spring comes and the ground warms up they sprout up again.

ANNUALS, such as lettuce and cucumber, make seeds and then die every year. Their seeds survive in the soil and then germinate the next year to produce new plants.

TREES AND SHRUBS are bigger plants that can't die back. Instead, in fall they suck their food down into their roots and drop their leaves so their bare woody branches can survive the frosts and wind.

What season is it?

Many plants recognize how long the days are, and then change how they grow. This helps them to know when to shut down for winter and when to start flowering. Imagine if there were a few very hot days in early spring. A plant that usually flowered in summer might think that summer had started and bloom, but none of the pollinating insects it needed would be around, and its flowers might die if it suddenly got cold again. By recognizing that the days are still short, the plant waits until the season is right before flowering.

Temperature

Not all plants can survive cold temperatures. Knowing the temperature each plant needs will help you grow them better. Many seeds need it to be very warm to germinate. For instance, pepper seeds don't like it much colder than 68°F (20°C), while lettuce won't germinate if it's much hotter than that. Cabbage plants that are used to colder climates will germinate as low as 39°F (4°C).

ZZZZZZZ

RHUBARB SLEEPING

Watch it, trying to sleep here!

SEEDS SLEEPING

Soil

The base of all life in your garden is the soil. Soil is a mixture of broken-down rocks, organic matter (living and dead plants and animals), air, and water. Soil is different all over the world, but whatever yours is like, you need to look after it if you want to have great fruits and vegetables to eat.

Ways you can harm soil

• Digging or walking on soil when it is wet can easily damage it.
• Digging deeply and turning the large clumps over will bury surface-loving animals deep down where they can't survive, and bring deep-living animals up to the surface, which they don't like either.
• Leaving soil bare, especially over the winter months, means the rain and wind can harm it.
• Weed killers and chemicals that kill insects and fungi will also kill your soil life. For a really healthy soil, keep it natural.

Show your soil some love

• Build organic matter into your soil by adding compost. Adding a lot of organic matter to your soil will help light soil to hold onto water and food, and make heavy soil drain better.
• Sow cover crops, such as clover and mustard, to provide a green cover when you're not growing a vegetable.
• Try a "no-dig" or "minimum-dig" system, where you just tickle the surface of the soil before sowing or planting. Just add compost to the soil surface and the worms will take it down deeper for you.

HOW DO I KNOW WHAT TYPE OF SOIL I HAVE?

We classify soil according to the size of the sand, silt, and clay particles in it. If your soil is a nice mixture of all three, we call it a "loam." Here's how to find out what soil type you have:

1. Fill a screw-top jar halfway with your soil, then fill to the top with water and screw the lid on tight.

2. Shake the jar hard for a couple of minutes and then let the soil settle for 24 hours.

3. The big sand particles will drop first, then the silt, and finally the tiny clay particles that form the top layer. Measure how wide each layer is to discover whether you have sandy, silty, or clay soil.

FACT

You can also measure your soil's pH—whether it is acidic or alkali. The ideal pH for soil is 6–7, but some plants such as blueberries prefer a more acidic pH of 4–5.5.

SANDY SOIL

0–10% CLAY
0–15% SILT
90–100% SAND

SILTY SOIL

7–27% CLAY
28–50% SILT
23–52% SAND

CLAY SOIL

40–100% CLAY
0–40% SILT
0–45% SAND

Compost magic

Soil and the creatures that live in it need food to keep them alive and healthy. In nature, plant and animal remains rot down to become "soil organic matter." Your garden needs organic matter, too, and the best way to give it this is to feed your soil good compost.

How is compost made?

There's some cool science behind composting, with a lot of microscopic bugs working at different temperatures to break down large pieces of plant waste into smaller and smaller parts until eventually it becomes "humus"—the name given to the sticky, rich, brown material that very old compost turns into.

Making compost is easy & fun

To make compost, all you really need is plant waste. Having a compost bin to put it in is not essential, but it helps keep it tidy. You can either buy one from a garden center or make your own from wood, such as old pallets. If you don't have a compost bin, then just pile your compost up under a plastic sheet to keep it dry.

FACT
You can compost any vegetable or fruit waste, coffee grounds, paper tea bags, and even human or pet hair. Don't compost meat, bread, pasta, or rice.

POLE BEANS & HOSES

Can you climb your way to the backyard gate, or will the hoses catch you out?

WHAT YOU WILL NEED

Pole Beans & Hoses is just like the game Shoots & Ladders. To play you will need a die and a counter for each player. Your counter could be anything that fits on one square of the board, such as a bottle top before you recycle it or perhaps a coin.

HOW TO PLAY

1. Starting on square number one, the aim is to be the first player to reach "home"—the backyard gate.

2. Roll the die to begin the game. The player who rolls the highest number moves their counter onto the board first.

3. Take turns to roll the die and move up the board following the numbers in sequence.

4. If your counter lands on a square at the bottom of a pole bean, you can "climb" up it and move your counter to the top. If your counter lands on a square at the top of a hose, your counter must slide down the hose to the square with the hose nozzle in it.

5. To win the game you need to roll the correct number to land on square 64.

Green & brown

To make good compost, you need to have a mixture of the following:

GREEN MATERIAL, such as kitchen waste and grass clippings, which has a high nitrogen content.

BROWN MATERIAL, such as straw, woodchips, or cardboard, which has more carbon in it. A good compost mix is one part green to three parts brown.

Layer the green and brown stuff as you make the pile so that they are evenly spread. You then just need to turn your compost pile every few weeks. This helps to get air into the pile to speed up the composting process. It also stops your compost from getting too hot—the bacteria that do the composting prefer it cool.

Not too wet, not too dry

If you don't have the right mixture of materials, then your compost heap might be either too wet or dry.

• If it's too wet and a little smelly, add some more brown material and turn it.

• If it's too dry, try adding some clippings or very green kitchen waste, or sprinkle it with water.

Don't panic or give up!

Even if you don't manage to make the best compost in the world, the rotten organic matter will still be good for your soil and plants. Let your pile sit for a year or so to make sure it is well-matured, and then spread it onto the soil before planting a hungry crop, such as potatoes or cabbages.

Stem, root, or fruit?

We grow different crops because they have particularly tasty or productive edible parts—but it's not the same part for every plant. We eat roots, stems, leaves, flowers, fruits, and seeds. Can you guess which part of its parent plant each of these vegetables is?

FOLLOW THE LINES TO FIND OUT WHICH PART OF THE PLANT YOU'RE REALLY EATING

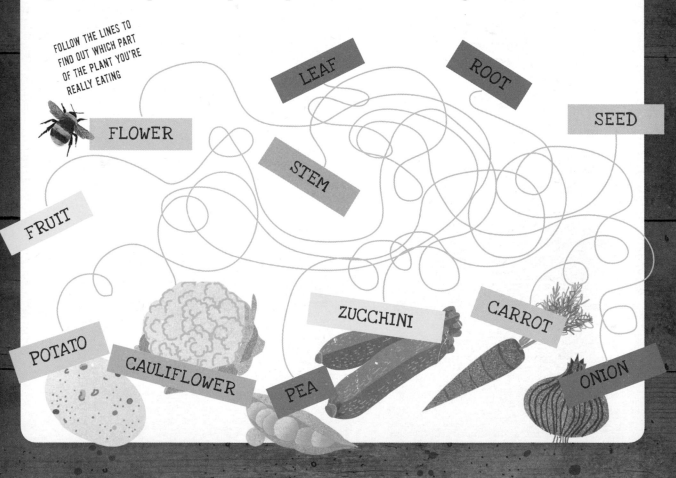

LEAF

ROOT

SEED

FLOWER

STEM

FRUIT

ZUCCHINI

CARROT

POTATO

CAULIFLOWER

PEA

ONION

Liquid fertilizer

COMFREY

Even if you have really good soil and add loads of rich compost, there are times when your plants need extra food. In a liquid fertilizer the plant can get a hold of nutrients immediately. You simply spray it onto the leaves or into the soil to be taken up by the roots.

Making your own

You can buy an organic fertilizer, but it's easy to make your own. Nettle or comfrey are great for this because they are full of the minerals your plants will need. Wear gloves—nettles sting and comfrey has itchy hairy leaves.

1. You'll need about 2 pounds (1 kg) of nettle or comfrey leaves. Cut them up a little so you can fit them into a bucket.

2. When the leaves are all in the bucket, fill it with water to about 2 inches (5 cm) from the top. Cover it to prevent rainwater from getting in—and to contain the stinky smell!

3. Let the mixture sit for four to six weeks and then it is ready to use.

You can pour your liquid fertilizer straight onto the soil, to be absorbed by your plants' roots. If you want to spray it onto plants, you will need to strain the liquid and add the old leaves and stems to the compost pile.

Yuck! That stinks!

NETTLES

Tools

There are some jobs you can do with bare hands, such as weeding and picking, but for most gardening tasks, you will need a tool. As you get good at gardening, you'll learn which tools suit which job—and the tools you like using best. To start you off, here are a dozen tools you can't do without.

SPADE OR SHOVEL For digging holes or for moving soil around.

FACT It's important to look after your tools and clean them after use.

TROWEL For planting your baby vegetable plants or for digging out weeds.

PITCHFORK Great for preparing soil for sowing or planting, and digging out weeds.

RAKES Use a normal garden rake for preparing a seedbed for sowing seeds. Use a "lawn" rake for clearing loose plant materials from grass or soil.

SIEVE To get any big lumps out of your compost.

Watch it with that rake!

HEALTH & SAFETY

Tools used in the wrong way, or without care, can be dangerous. For younger children, most tools should be used under close supervision. Look for good-quality child-sized rakes, spades, and pitchforks—adult ones are almost impossible to use effectively and will result in injury to either the user or anyone else who gets within range. Always wear sturdy footwear in the garden. Also learn how to properly sharpen knives, hoes, and garden shears. It is an important skill that will make the tools work better.

HOE Fantastic for quick weeding.

WHEELBARROW For moving heavy stuff—and they're fun for riding around in, too!

GARDEN SHEARS Big scissors that can cut through big plants and stems.

WATERING CANS A big one for watering big plants, and a small one for your seedlings in flowerpots. It's also important to have a "rose" for the spout.

SCISSORS OR A POCKET KNIFE For cutting twine and other small things.

BUCKET For carrying small things around.

DIBBLE A pointed stick that you use to make holes in the ground for planting.

What's a weed?

PRETTY TOO

A weed is often described as a plant in the wrong place. For some gardeners, they are the enemy that must be destroyed, but you can think of them as beautiful friends who can help in the garden.

Weeds for covering the ground

In organic gardening, bare soil is not good. If you have ground not ready for planting, you can put in a temporary crop such as mustard or buckwheat—called a "green manure." Or you can let the weeds come in and do the job for you. This green cover will hold onto nutrients that plants need, and stop the soil from being ruined by rain, wind, and heavy boots.

Weeds for wildlife

It is good to encourage a lot of insects and birds into your garden because they will help pollinate plants and eat pests. A great way to attract them is to have wild plants (or weeds) that they like, especially if you let them flower.

Weeds for food

Weeds are very good at getting a hold of nutrients. Some, like dandelions and chicory, have big long roots that can grow down 6 feet (2 m) or more into the soil and bring up nutrients that you can then use for growing your crops.

YOU CAN EVEN EAT MANY WEEDS. GOUTWEED, DANDELION LEAF, AND LAMB'S-QUARTERS ARE ALL PERFECTLY GOOD TO EAT.

How to get rid of weeds

Although weeds can help your garden, there are some times when you have to pull them out. Here's how to deal with them:

DEEP-ROOTED PERENNIALS, such as bindweed, dock, and thistle. Dig down and try to remove as much root as possible. You'll need to do this a few times as the plant regrows, but eventually they will die. If you have a patch without crops you can try covering it with cardboard or plastic mulch for six months or more. This slows down the weed growth and brings the roots nearer the surface, making it easier to pull them up.

QUICK-GROWING ANNUALS, such as lamb's-quarters. These weeds love bare ground and germinate quickly. The best way to control them is to use a hoe as soon as you see the tiny plants. If you wait until they are bigger, their roots will have taken hold and removing them will take more effort. If you let them get too big, you could pull a vegetable up at the same time by mistake.

If I just lean a little further...

FACT
Dandelions are great for wildlife. Bees eat the pollen, beetles can shelter under the leaves, and some birds eat the seeds.

Sowing seeds

Watching a seed germinate and grow into a plant is one of the best things. It's not hard to get a plant to grow as long as you have good fresh seeds and give it a good start.

Flowerpots or soil?

For most vegetables, you can either sow seeds straight into the ground, or put them first into flowerpots or seed-starting trays and then transplant them into the soil when they are bigger. For plants such as peppers that need warm temperatures, you'll need to sow them inside and then plant them in the garden or greenhouse when the weather gets hotter. Other crops, such as lettuce, need to be grown a little larger before planting outdoors to help them get ahead of the weeds and pests. Some plants, such as carrots, do not like being transplanted, so you always sow them straight into soil.

How very kind of you ...

START ME IN A POT ...

SOW ME DIRECT

... THEN PLANT ME OUT

SOWING IN THE GROUND

1. First rake the soil to make a fine texture or "tilth." If the soil has big lumps, when the root comes out of the seed it may just find a big air gap and not be able to survive.

2. Create a trench or "drill" in the soil with a stick or a hoe. As a general rule, seeds like being as deep in the soil as they are big, so your drill should be very shallow.

3. If the soil is very dry, water the drill before sowing (if you do it afterward it may wash all of your seeds away).

4. Sow your seeds along the length of the drill—spacing will depend on the plant you are growing.

5. Cover the seeds with a thin covering of fine soil. If you have very heavy or sticky soil then you can instead cover them with a peat-free compost, which the young seedlings will find easier to grow through.

6. Write a label with the name of the fruit or vegetable and the date sown.

HOW WARM DOES IT NEED TO BE?

Good average temperature for warm seasonal vegetables, such as beans, sweet corn, cucumbers, and squash.

Good average temperature for cool seasonal vegetables such as plants in the cabbage family, lettuce, onions, peas, and spinach.

Minimum germination temperature for squash, peppers, sweet corn, eggplant, and cucumber.

Minimum germination temperature for tomatoes and French beans.

Minimum germination temperature for onions and parsnips.

39°F — 4°C
50°F — 10°C
54°F — 12°C
59°F — 15.5°C
61°F — 16°C
68–77°F — 20–25°C
70°F — 21°C
75°F — 24°C
81°F — 27°C

Minimum germination temperature for plants in the cabbage family, beets, and peas.

Ideal germination temperature for broad beans.

Temperature at which ladybugs come out in spring, although day length is also a factor.

Best average germination temperature for most vegetables.

Temperature at which spinach and lettuce often start producing seeds, although nighttime temperature and day length also influence this.

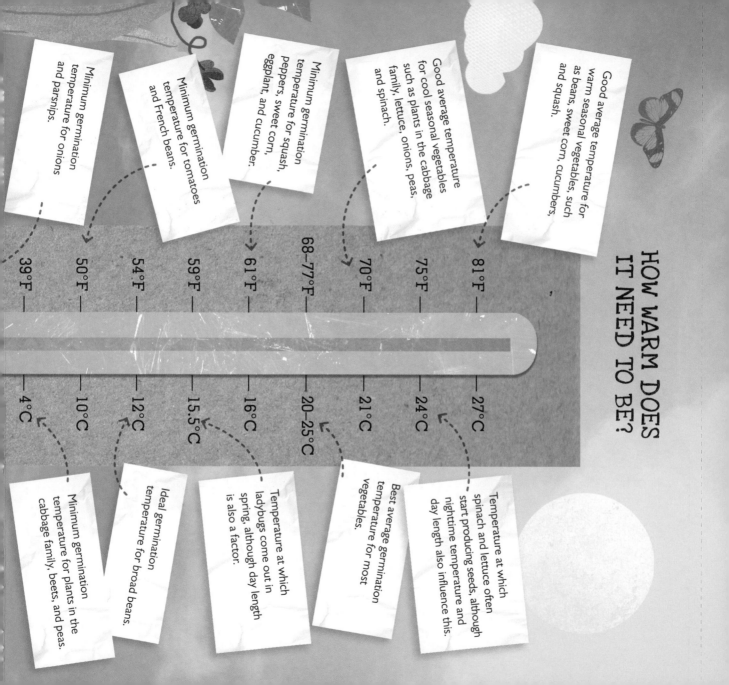

Temperature at which which the hardiest Siberian kales can still survive.

Temperature below which some plants in the cabbage family will suffer, such as broccoli and less hardy cabbages.

Temperature at which your tender plants, such as beans, cucumbers, eggplant, tomato, sweet corn, and squash, will be safe in an unheated tunnel.

-4°F
10°F
25°F
28°F
30°F
32°F
36°F

-20°C
-12°C
-4°C
-2°C
-1°C
0°C
2°C

Temperature below which most kales will suffer.

Temperature at which some half-hardy plants will suffer, such as globe artichokes, beets, carrots, celery, and chard.

Temperature at which tender plants will usually die, unless protected.

SOWING IN FLOWERPOTS OR TRAYS

The basic principle is the same as soil, except you are sowing seeds into a seed compost.

1. Fill a flowerpot or seed-starting tray with compost and firm it gently—try using the bottom of another flowerpot to do this.

2. Water the compost a little if dry—use a small watering can with a "rose" on the spout.

3. Sprinkle the seeds on the top of the flowerpot or tray.

4. Cover the seeds with a thin layer of compost.

5. Write a label with the name of the fruit or vegetable and date sown.

You have to be a little careful with watering with this method. The compost needs to stay moist but not wet. You can cover the flowerpots or trays with a plastic sheet or plastic wrap, but make sure you take it off as soon as you see the seedlings, otherwise they may get diseases from the damp air.

Hardening off seedlings

If you have sown your plants indoors in flowerpots or trays, you'll be eager to get them out into the garden as soon as possible. But be careful! Your baby plants are not ready to go straight out. Even hardy vegetables such as cabbages won't be so hardy if grown under cover. They are used to being warm and dry and out of the wind. You will need to get them gradually used to the outdoors.

The easiest way is to take them outdoors during the day starting with an hour or two and leading up to full days. Do this for a week or two, bringing them back inside at night. It's also worth reducing watering during this period because this will toughen the plant a little. If you have an unheated greenhouse, you can put them in there instead and leave them overnight. Traditionally, cold frames were used for this purpose, and if you have the space they are great. You just lift the lid during the day and close it up at night.

If you really want to get your plants into the ground, you can use an old plastic bottle with the bottom cut off to cover them at night. Make sure you remove the bottle during the day because it can get really hot in a bottle when the sun is out.

Now, how can I get in there ...

Transplanting

So, you have sown your seeds into a flowerpot or seed-starting tray, and now they're ready to move outdoors. What's the best way to transplant them into the garden to make sure they grow well?

Bare root transplants

This is the term given to baby plants that you pull up from where you sowed them. Use a trowel or blunt knife (depending on the size of the seedling) to lift up the plantlets from under their roots, as you gently pull them from the top. For very small seedlings, you should hold the leaf, not the stem, to avoid crushing it.

Decide where you want the plant to finally grow and make a hole there big enough to hold the roots of the seedling. Then lower the baby plant into it and gently push the soil in around the roots.

Choose the healthiest and strongest seedlings to transplant. It's a good idea to plant a few in flowerpots as backups in case the ones you plant outside get eaten or die.

I'm the champion of champions!

1.

2.

3.

Potting on before transplanting

It sometimes happens that you need to pot on your seedlings before you plant them out. This can happen if you have sown inside and then the weather is too bad to plant out.

You can plant your bare root seedlings or plants into a bigger flowerpot (using the same principles as planting into soil) and grow them bigger until the time is right to get them into their final place.

Cell transplants

Transplanting from seed-starting trays divided into cells is easier. Just push the plant and ball of soil out of the tray and plant it into the ground.

Usually, you would have just one seedling in each cell, but for some crops—scallions and beets, for example—you might sow a few in each. If you have more plants in the cell than you need, you can always pinch off the weaker seedlings without disturbing the soil ball.

No water for me, please!

FACT
Always give your plants a good drink after you've transplanted them to help settle the soil around the roots. You could use a liquid fertilizer (see page 17) to give them a boost.

Harvesting fruits & vegetables

Unless you camp outside in the yard all summer long to eat straight from the plants, you'll need to pick food to bring indoors for cooking. You also want your winter crops to last as long as possible. Here's how to get great-tasting crops to last longer all year round:

Spring & summer

• Unless you can pick 5 minutes before cooking, try to get into the garden first thing in the morning. Vegetables take up water during the night when the air is cooler and damper. This means that they are full of water first thing in the morning and will last longer when picked.

• Vegetables don't like being hot! The quicker you can get them into a refrigerator or a cool room after picking, the longer they will last.

• How big do you like your vegetables: baby beans and tiny turnips, or massive marrows and enormous eggplants? Plants can grow very quickly during the summer, so keep checking and picking regularly.

FACT
Avoid leaving vegetables out in the sun while you're picking them.

Phew, it's so hot!

Fall & winter

• How cold is your garden? Most hardy root crops will cope better if it is a little colder. In wet climates with winters where it's warmer than 40°F (5°C), you may be better off digging root crops up to avoid them being eaten by slugs or damaged by rot. In cold conditions, below 15°F (-9°C), you will need to add extra protection. Straw or floating row covers are often used.

• Most leafy crops, including leeks, are best left in the soil until you need to harvest them. Watch out though—birds love these tasty snacks in winter when there is not much else around to eat. Put a floating row cover or net over your crop to protect it, but make sure you take it off if there's a lot of snow, because it can pile up on top of the net and the weight of it can crush the plants underneath.

• Carrots and parsnips build up sugar in their roots, which works as a natural antifreeze, stopping them from being damaged. Traditionally, these crops are covered with a thick layer of straw, which helps to protect them and also makes them easier to dig up if you have long periods of frost. You can also dig them up and store them in a box of soil or sand in a cool garage or shed.

Guys, it's really cold over here!

Planning your vegetable plot

Now that we've looked at how to grow your own fruits and vegetables from seeds, it's time to work out which ones to put in your plot and where they all fit.

What is rotation?

"Rotation" is the word gardeners use to describe how they grow different crops in different places each year. Moving plants around—growing beans in a bed or part of a bed one year, and potatoes in the same space the next year—helps to reduce pests and diseases. Some plants are also good at smothering weeds, and if you give them a turn in every bed, you can stop weeds from taking over. And because different plants need varying quantities of minerals, you can balance their food needs by growing them in a different spot each year.

Plant families

The easiest way to group plants is by family. For example, cabbage, cauliflower, and radish are all part of the cabbage family, while onions, leeks, and garlic are *Alliums*.

A basic rotation plan involves dividing your growing space into four and changing the crop in each part each year, so you have a four-year cycle or rotation.

So what should I grow?

The next few pages offer some ideas, but start by choosing vegetables you like eating, and then think about which types taste better picked fresh or can be difficult to find at the store. Leafy crops, such as lettuce, spinach, and herbs, usually grow fast and easily, and if you choose potatoes or tomatoes, you can grow unusual kinds that you can't buy. If you have space, you can keep one bed as a "ley" each year. This means that you plant a green crop, such as clover. It isn't to eat; instead, when it starts to die back at the end of the growing season, you simply dig it back into the soil to enrich it.

The top ten vegetables

There's a lot to think about when choosing what to grow in your vegetable plot. To help you plan, here are ten vegetables that are great to eat and not too difficult to grow. Try them, and don't be disappointed if they don't grow perfectly the first time—just try them again or try a different one the next year.

1. Carrots

Sow carrot seeds directly into the soil. You'll eventually need about 2 inches (5 cm) between plants, but not all the seeds will germinate, so you can sow more thickly and then remove some of the seedlings once they have germinated.

Carrots need weeding. Learn to recognize baby carrot leaves (see right) to make sure you don't pull them up by mistake. You'll need to water your carrots if it's dry.

To see if your carrots are ready to eat, you can either pull one up and look at it or just loosen the soil around the top of the root. You can eat carrots at any age, but the longer you leave them, the more you get.

3. Potatoes

Potatoes are really easy to grow. Keep the potatoes in a light, warm place until they sprout a little. Then plant them in the soil about 6 inches (15 cm) down. As the leaves grow up you can move some soil from between the plants to cover the new growth. Do this a couple of times and then let the leaves grow up. The plants need a lot of water as the potatoes get bigger. Dig down for your treasure as soon as the potatoes flower or the leaves start dying back.

2. Beets

Beets are the most colorful of vegetables. Most beets are bright red, and make food (and your pee!) pink. Sow one beet "seed" (which actually contains three or four real seeds) straight into the soil about 4 inches (10 cm) apart. Let them all grow until big enough to pull up. You can eat them at almost any size, but they get a little tough if they stay in the soil too long. The leaves can be eaten, too, like spinach.

4. Pumpkins

Pumpkins are more difficult to grow but a lot of fun—as well as eating them you can make them into Halloween jack-o'-lanterns! They like it warm to germinate, around 60–70°F (15–21°C), so put them in a flowerpot inside on a windowsill. Plant the seedling outside when you know there won't be a frost. They also like plenty of compost and water. To know whether your pumpkin is ready, just push your fingernail gently into the skin—if it leaves a mark, it's not ready.

PUMPKIN PATCH

5. Peas

Peas are simple to grow and taste so good straight from the pod! They germinate even when it's cool so are a great early crop. Mice and other rodents like to eat the seeds, so try sowing into seed-starting trays and transplanting. The plants need to be about 3 inches (7.5 cm) apart. For sowing into the soil outdoors, cover with 2 inches (5 cm) of soil. Sow in double rows 6 inches (15 cm) apart. You can use twiggy branches for the plants to climb through and up. Check the seed packet to find out the final height of the plant—it's usually about 3 feet (1 m), but some pea plants can reach 5 feet (1.5 m).

PINCHING OFF

If you let most tomato plants grow naturally, they get out of control. You will still get fruit on them, but it makes it difficult to pick (or even get into the greenhouse). To keep them under control, you pinch off the side shoots so that the plant grows straight and puts its energy into producing yummy fruit for you.

SIDE SHOOTS

FACT
Tomatoes are actually a fruit, not a vegetable!

6. Tomatoes

Tomatoes like an early start and a long growing season. Seed packets will often say (in days) how long it takes for the plant to produce fruit. If you live in a colder part of the world, choose the lowest number of days that you can.

Sow in early spring. You may need to transplant the seedlings to a bigger flowerpot at least once before transplanting after the last frost, either in a greenhouse or outside. Allow 2 feet (60 cm) between each plant. Bushy "determinate" tomato plants can be left to grow as they are, but "indeterminate" tomato plants need training and pinching.

6.

7. Beans

There are hundreds of different beans that grow as bushy beans and climbing pole beans. Let's talk about the climbers because it's neat to see how tall they can grow! Pole beans don't like frost, so sow indoors in mid- to late spring, or directly into the soil after the last frost. Plant them 2 inches (5 cm) deep in double rows 18 inches (45 cm) apart, with 9 inches (22.5 cm) between plants. Water well, especially when the beans are forming. They need at least 6 feet (almost 2 m) of stake or twine to climb, and may need to be tied to this when very young.

8. Sweet corn

This vegetable takes up a lot of space, and you need to grow a few in a block to make sure they germinate well. Sow them directly into the soil or plant transplants outside, after the last frost, in a square with 18 inches (45 cm) between plants in both directions. Plant two seeds at each point, and then remove the weaker seedling if they both germinate.

Water well if it's dry. You'll know the corn is ready when the tassels turn brown and die.

7.

8.

9.

10.

9. Lettuce

There is a huge range of shapes and colors to choose from, including some that are hardy for colder climates. Most lettuce plants do well sown from early spring. Sow in a seed-starting tray, with or without cells, and then transplant into the ground 6–12 inches (15–30 cm) apart, depending on the size of the lettuce. You can also sow them more thickly and cut them when they are small for baby leafy greens. In dry, hot weather, you will need to water them a lot for a good crop.

10. Kale

Kale is a great source of vitamin C in the winter and is delicious steamed like spinach or drizzled with oil and toasted in the oven until crispy.

Sow in seed-starting trays and then transplant into the soil 3 feet (1 m) apart. Sow in later spring or early summer so that the plant is a good size by wintertime. It will withstand severe frosts and even keep growing in temperatures just above freezing. "Tuscan Black" or the hardy "Russian Red" are good kale plants to try.

Yum! Lettuce is my favorite.

The top three fruits

Eating fruits from the tree or bush is simply the best! There are a lot of fruit trees you can grow, but we're mostly looking here at smaller plants that you can harvest, even if you're not very tall.

1. Strawberries

Strawberries are really easy plants to grow. You can sow the tiny "Alpine" ones from seeds in the early spring (they will grow in even really poor soil), or buy the plants with bigger fruits and grow them either in the ground or in flowerpots. Strawberries only need about 1 square foot (900 cm^2) for each plant. They like plenty of food, so make sure you add compost to the soil before planting. It's also a good idea to put some straw or other soil covering around the plants. It will stop splashing when it rains, which keeps the fruits dry and stops them from rotting.

FRUIT PAIRS GAME

Find the matching fruit cards to win. You will need two players.

1. Lay out the cards facedown. For an easy game, lay them in a grid, or do it randomly to make it a little more difficult.

2. The youngest player goes first by choosing a card and carefully turning it over. Try not to move any of the other cards near it. The player then turns another card over. If the two cards match, they keep the pair and go again.

3. If the cards don't match, the first player turns them back over and the next player goes. You need to remember which card is where in case you turn over the other matching fruit.

You've won if you have the most pairs when all the fruits are matched!

FRUIT PAIRS GAME

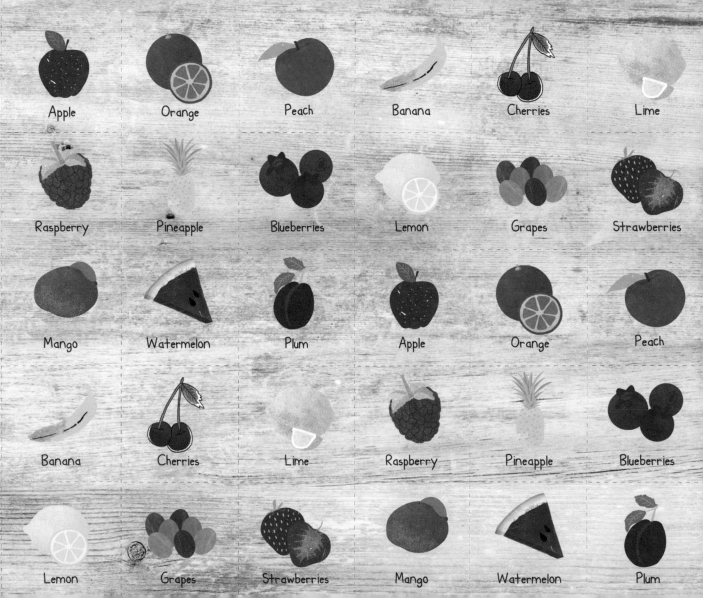

Apple

Orange

Peach

Banana

Cherries

Lime

Raspberry

Pineapple

Blueberries

Lemon

Grapes

Strawberries

Mango

Watermelon

Plum

Apple

Orange

Peach

Banana

Cherries

Lime

Raspberry

Pineapple

Blueberries

Lemon

Grapes

Strawberries

Mango

Watermelon

Plum

2. Raspberries

You'll need more space for raspberries because they grow to 5 or 6 feet (1.5–1.8 m) and like to spread out. Grow them in rows with 18 inches (45 cm) between plants. You need a stake at each end of the row with three wires stretched between them to tie the "canes" into as they grow. Or you can tie two canes to a single stake, planting one on each side. There are summer and fall raspberries. Fall-bearing plants are a little easier to look after and give a bigger crop.

3.

2.

This cake is all for me!

3. Blueberries

The main thing you need to know about blueberries is that they like acidic soil. However, you can still grow them if your soil is not acidic, because they really like growing in containers. You'll need a big flowerpot, ideally 2 feet (60 cm) in diameter, but you can use a smaller one when the plants are young. Blueberries need to be kept watered in dry conditions—try to use rainwater if you can because tap water may be alkaline.

Saving Seeds

It's very easy to buy seeds, and you can grow great vegetables from them, but it's also a lot of fun to save your own seeds from plants you've grown yourself. You just need to know a little about how different plants pollinate to make sure you get the seeds you want.

The male & female

As we saw on page 7, plants need both the male and female parts of the flower to make seeds. Some plants have these in the same flower (such as the pea plant); some have them on different flowers on the same plant (such as zucchini); others have separate male and female plants.

ASPARAGUS HAS SEPARATE MALE AND FEMALE PLANTS.

Keeping it real—or getting "true" seeds

If you want your seeds to grow into the same variety as the one you took the seeds from (or "true"), there are a few things that you need to do:

• Grow from an "open-pollinated" variety. Make sure the seed packet doesn't say "F1" or "hybrid" on it.

• Either grow only one variety of the vegetable you want seeds from, or keep your plants separate from other varieties of that vegetable that are in your garden (or even in your neighbor's yard.)

• Finally, you have to make sure that the flowers actually get pollinated. Plants have different ways of doing this in nature. Sweet corn is pollinated by wind, but most plants get insects to do the job for them. To get true seeds from some plants, you may even need to pollinate by hand.

HAND-POLLINATING

All you need are clothespins and some labels or sticks for identifying the plants you've pollinated.

ZUCCHINI & OTHER SQUASH

MALE

FEMALE

FEMALE FLOWER

MALE FLOWER

1. One evening, just before it gets dark, find a couple of male and female flowers on each plant that are just about to open. Put a clothespin over the end of them to stop them from opening.

Hang on, pollinating is my job!

2. First thing the next morning, pick one of the male flowers and carefully peel the petals off. Using the stamen inside as a paintbrush, rub the pollen onto the inside of the female flower on a different plant. Repeat this with the other male flowers.

3. Close the female flowers again with a clothespin (this stops bees from getting in), label them, and wait for the fruits to mature and ripen.

FACT
Peas and tomatoes are easy to save seeds from, whereas cauliflower and broccoli are more difficult.

Harvesting & storing seeds

OK, so we know how to grow the right seeds, but what's the best way of harvesting and keeping them? Every plant is different, but here are a few basic rules that apply to most of them. Once you get the seed-saving bug, you'll want to learn about each vegetable to know exactly what to do.

Which plants to pick from

You should choose the best seeds from the best plants. Look for healthy, strong plants that have the characteristics you want. So if your beans have red flowers, make sure all the plants you save seeds from have red flowers. Do a family taste test to make sure you are choosing the tastiest plants.

ALL THE STAGES OF POLE BEANS, FROM FLOWER TO RIPE POD

When to pick

The seeds need to be ripe. The longer you leave them on the plant to ripen, the better. However, if it rains a lot where you live, they might turn moldy before they ripen. For some vegetables (such as lettuce) you can pick the whole plant and hang it in a dry place. Place the seed head in a bag (or put a newspaper underneath) so you don't lose the seeds.

We've bean looking everywhere for this ...

Checking the seeds

You should save only the very best seeds, so check what you pick really carefully. Throw out any broken or moldy seeds. You'll also need to get rid of any pieces of twig, seed coating, or leaf that might be hanging around with the seeds. They are mostly lighter than the seeds, so you can put everything in a shallow bowl and blow on it very, very gently. All the debris will fly away, leaving clean seeds in the bowl.

How to store the seeds

The drier you get your seeds, the longer they will keep. Don't be tempted to stick them in an oven to dry, however, as high temperatures can kill them. Just store them in a warm, dry room. Once dry, you need to keep them in a dark, cool, and dry place. Sealing them in a plastic container works well. You can even put them into the refrigerator!

I'll help you eat the tomatoes!

FACT
Wet seeds need to be washed and dried on a plate first to stop them from rotting.

CLEANING TOMATO SEEDS

Tomato seeds are covered in a gelatin that stops germination until the conditions are right. So to save the seeds, you've got to remove them from the tomato and "ferment" them to break down the gelatin.

1. Let the seeds sit in some water in a jar for a few days until the mixture becomes a little smelly.

2. Pour the mixture into a strainer and rinse really well with cold water. This will clean off the fermented gelatin.

3. Lay the seeds out on a plate, making sure they aren't touching, or they will stick together. Put the plate onto a windowsill until totally dry, which may take a few days.

Plants not grown from seeds

It is not always easy to gather the right kind of seeds from some fruits, especially perennial plants, such as rhubarb and fruit trees. But don't worry, we can still produce more of these plants (this is called "propagation"). Here's how:

STRAWBERRIES

Suckers

Raspberries send out suckers (or young shoots) from under the ground. You don't always want these because they can get in the way of other plants and paths, but if you want new raspberry plants, they are just what you need. Get a spade, dig them up, and plant them in a new place.

Runners

Who doesn't love strawberries? Here's a really easy way to get a lot more plants: In late summer, the plant will grow long stems called "runners" along the top of the soil. At the end of each runner is a baby plant. Put this baby plant into the soil or a flowerpot while it is still attached to the mother. It will grow roots, and you can then cut the runner and you will have another plant.

FACT
Selling plants that aren't needed is a great way to top up your allowance!

RASPBERRIES

Tip rooting

Blackberries send out powerful shoots that can easily grow 2 inches (5 cm) a day in the spring. When the shoots get too long to hold themselves up, they droop down to the ground, and when the growing tip reaches the soil, it grows roots and forms a new plant. You can then dig up this plant, cut off the old stem, and plant it somewhere else.

BLACKBERRIES

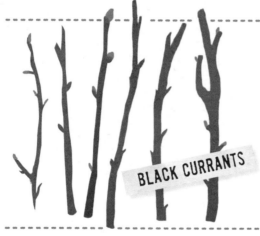

BLACK CURRANTS

Cuttings

Black currants are super easy to propagate. You just cut a short length of 8–10 inches (20–25 cm) of young wood and stick it in the ground in late winter or early spring (just before it starts sprouting leaves). It will then form roots and turn into a new plant. You might find that not all your cuttings work, so always do a few more than you need.

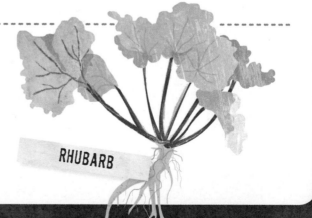

RHUBARB

Dividing

This is probably the easiest way of getting more plants. It works well for almost all perennial plants that grow in clumps, such as rhubarb. Just dig up the plant and cut it up into smaller pieces with a spade. Replant the smaller parts and they will each grow into a new plant.

Fruits & vegetables in pots

We've talked a lot about soil in this book, but don't worry if you don't have any or if you don't have a vegetable plot. Absolutely everyone can grow something! Let's have a look at some plants you can grow in flowerpots, from little herbs right up to juicy strawberries.

Herbs

Herbs are great for flowerpots. For indoors, try cilantro, basil, and parsley. For outdoors, sage, rosemary, chives, oregano, and mint are all easy to grow and pretty hardy.

Leafy greens

Most leafy greens are easy to grow in flowerpots either inside or outside. Try growing four different types of greens and then mix them all together:

ARUGULA Very quick to germinate and perfect in a salad or on a pizza.

MIZUNA Spiky-leaved, quick-growing green from the cabbage family.

RED MUSTARD Great color and slightly spicy. Watch out—the leaves get very hot and spicy when they are older!

"SALAD BOWL" Comes in red or green and works well as baby leaf, but it also tastes great when big.

FACT

Keep your herbs on the kitchen windowsill or just outside the back door, ready for when you are doing the cooking.

Vegetables

Vegetables with smaller roots do better in flowerpots than those with big deep roots (such as parsnips) or those that need a lot of water (such as cabbages). Try scallions, radishes, carrots, leeks, fennel, or beets to start with. You can sow most of them in a flowerpot, or you can grow as seedlings and transplant (for all but the radishes and carrots). If you don't get much rain where you live, then you will need to water them most days.

Fruits

The easiest fruits to grow in flowerpots are strawberries. They don't need much room, and as long as you water them enough, they will do really well. Growing in flowerpots also helps keep slugs away! If you find a trailing plant, you can grow it around the edge of a flowerpot with something else planted in the middle.

Grow your own pizzas!

Basic pizza dough is really easy to make (and delicious to eat), but a homemade pizza is especially satisfying if all the vegetables you use for toppings have been picked straight from your own backyard.

The key to most pizza toppings is a thick tomato sauce. If you eat a lot of pizza (or pasta), choose a beefsteak or plum tomato to make the sauce with. They'll ensure it has loads of flavor. If you've also grown some little cherry tomatoes, you can use them whole on the top of your pizza.

Toppings you can grow

TOMATOES The large plum or beefsteak types make the best sauce, but any tomatoes will taste good when they're cooked down slowly and thoroughly.

ONIONS You can use any type of onion, even small scallions. Use chopped into the tomato sauce and as a topping, too, sliced finely and added to the pizza before it's cooked.

ZUCCHINI A great extra to add to the classic tomato/onion/basil mix. Slice them thin on top of the tomato layer.

Just one or two plants are often enough in the garden. Once they get going, they produce non-stop, and in lavish quantities, throughout the growing season.

HERBS The classic pizza herbs are basil and oregano, both of which are easy to grow. Oregano is a tough herb that you can grow in a flowerpot or almost any corner of the garden. Cut it back regularly to make sure that the leaves stay small and tasty. Basil is less hardy. If you live in a cool climate, try it in flowerpots on a sunny windowsill, or in a greenhouse.

MAKING YOUR PIZZAS

MAKING THE PIZZA DOUGH

Make your dough at least a couple of hours before you want to cook your pizza. This recipe makes enough dough for four individual pizzas.

- 2 cups (300 g) bread flour
- 1 teaspoon active dry yeast
- 1 cup (200 ml) lukewarm water
- Pinch of salt
- 1 tablespoon olive oil

1. Put all of the ingredients into a large bowl and stir until the mixture makes a firm but soft dough. Cover the bowl with plastic wrap and let rest for 15 minutes.

2. Use your fingers to fold the edges of the dough into the center about ten times, then cover again and let rest for 15 minutes.

3. Repeat the step twice, and then rest the dough until it doubles in size. You can even make the dough the day before and put it in the refrigerator to rise slowly.

4. Divide the dough into four pieces. Knead each one briefly, then use plenty of flour and a rolling pin to roll each piece into a circle, getting the dough as thin as you can.

5. Your pizzas are now ready for the toppings.

MAKING THE TOMATO SAUCE

Get the tomato sauce cooked while your pizza dough is rising.

- 2 large onions (or 4 small onions)
- 1 pound (450 g) large tomatoes
- 2 tablespoons olive oil
- 1 teaspoon brown sugar

1. Finely chop the onions and put them in a saucepan with the oil. Cook over low heat for 10 minutes or until soft.

2. Chop the tomatoes, and add to the pan with the onions. Add the sugar, and cook slowly over medium heat for about 40 minutes until the sauce is sticky and jamlike. Place your baking sheets in the oven, and preheat the oven to 425°F (220°C).

PUTTING IT TOGETHER

1. Lay the dough pieces for the pizzas on aluminum foil and spread a layer of tomato sauce on each.

2. Add thinly sliced onion or zucchini (or both) and a generous sprinkle of basil or oregano (or both). Don't forget to finish off with some mozzarella cheese or grated parmesan.

3. Place the pizzas on the foil straight onto the hot baking sheets in the oven; they'll be ready in 10–15 minutes. Yum!

Who needs lettuce when there's PIZZA on the menu?

Index

Picture credits
Shutterstock: Main book: 6, 13,
15, 17, 20, 22, 23, 24, 30, 31, 32,
33, 34, 35, 36, 37, 38, 41, 47.
Extras: sowing seeds pull-out
(soil); plant nutrients (twine).

Kiddish font courtesy of Matt
Bruinooge.

AUTHOR'S ACKNOWLEDGMENTS
For Max & Sam
Thanks to Ruth for
making it all possible, Ivan
and Jonah for their
constant inspiration, and
Monica for the ongoing
encouragement.